A Way
in the
Wilderness

KELLEY KILLIAN

WESTBOW
PRESS®
A DIVISION OF THOMAS NELSON
& ZONDERVAN

WestBow Press books may be ordered through booksellers or by contacting:

WestBow Press
A Division of Thomas Nelson & Zondervan
1663 Liberty Drive
Bloomington, IN 47403
www.westbowpress.com
844-714-3454

ISBN: 979-8-3850-1783-6 (sc)
ISBN: 979-8-3850-1784-3 (hc)
ISBN: 979-8-3850-1785-0 (e)

Library of Congress Control Number: 2024901775

Print information available on the last page.

WestBow Press rev. date: 02/27/2024

I AM MAKING A WAY IN THE WILDERNESS.
—Isaiah 43:19

Dedication

For Courtney Ragland Gresham
Thank you for challenging me to write with honesty, truth, and love.
I will love you forever, sweet girl.

Special Thanks

To Woods Michael Killian
Someday, my sweet boy, Nana will tell you the story
of all the ways the Lord worked through you to make
sure this book was completed. Thank you.
Nana loves you.

CONTENTS

Book I: Recognize

Book II: Assess and Equip

BOOK I

Recognize

ONE

A Storm is Coming

I have always been fascinated by the sea. The adventurousness, the unexpectedness, and certainly the uncontrollable vastness of the ocean are both breathtakingly beautiful and terrifying at the same time. So is life, I suppose. We could also describe our life experiences at times as adventurous, unexpected, and perhaps even out of control.

If we venture out into the deep parts of the sea, there is no surviving it unless we are prepared with what is needed to keep us from sinking or being swept away by either visible storms or invisible currents that move beneath the surface. A couple of years ago, I read the book *Adrift: A True Story of Love, Loss, and Survival at Sea.* It is about a twenty-four-year-old woman and her fiancé who were making a voyage across the Pacific Ocean from Tahiti to San Diego to deliver a sailing boat. She became stranded alone in the middle of the ocean after her fiancé was swept overboard during a fierce hurricane. She survived for forty days. Not only did she survive, but she navigated—with only a few key pieces of equipment—what was left of her sailing vessel hundreds of miles to Hawaii using the knowledge and skills she had learned prior to the voyage. She had no high-tech navigation system or electronics of any kind because all the gadgets that would have made for a quick rescue had been swept overboard or destroyed by the high winds and crashing waves.[1]

Had she left all the responsibility of navigating a vessel on the open sea to those gadgets or to someone else, she would not have been able to accomplish what she did and probably would not have survived. In the end, this young lady had to depend on her own preparatory work before the storm hit.

Storms at sea have no limits except what God places on them (Job 38:8–10). The waves are so high and so powerful that poorly built vessels cannot withstand the pressure. Neither can we withstand the pressure and destruction of life's storms unless we are prepared ahead of time for what may come against us and have a rock-solid foundation to anchor us. This book is intended to help you dig deep and build a foundation that promotes turning up the heat of our hearts for Christ so we are prepared and better able to withstand the storms that could cause us to stumble or lose our way.

Moreover, a storm is coming. The Bible says that in the last days, some will abandon the faith, follow deceivers, and be led away by those who do wrong (1 Timothy 4:1). We are to be careful so we will not fall from our strong faith (2 Peter 3:17). In the coming storm, we believers must be prepared so we can withstand it with our faith intact.

---

[1] Tami Oldham Ashcraft, *Adrift* (HarperCollins Publishers Inc., Digital Edition May 2018), chap 5. Kindle.

TWO

Warning Signs

The National Weather Service (NWS) is responsible for issuing warnings in the event of gale-force winds, which include a sustained wind force of thirty-four to forty-seven knots for more than ten minutes. These gale warnings allow mariners to take precautionary actions to ensure their safety at sea or to seek safe anchorage and ride out the storm on land.[2] Gale warning flags are raised, and alerts are broadcasted by the NWS to warn people of the dangers with these winds.

With the storm headed our way, we should raise a warning flag now for the church to be aware of and prepare for the arrival of several groups or categories of deceivers that bring the storm with them. They bring the winds of confusion and deception taking direct aim at believers in Christ. The Bible warns us in 2 Corinthians 11 of their coming and the possibility that we might be led astray from our sincere and pure devotion to Christ.

---

[2]   Wikipedia, s.v. "Gale warning," last modified November 13, 2023, https://en.wikipedia.org/wiki/Gale_warning.

In its simplest form, that is what this book is about; it is a warning sign, a red flag, a call for preparation and a watchful eye. Just like sailors preparing for unexpected storms, believers in Christ must also be prepared so we will not only survive but thrive, which is God's intention for the church.

Interestingly, the Bible makes it clear we are to grow up into our salvation and we are to practice our faith in our everyday lives. This includes practicing righteousness, honorable thinking, and love. Part of being prepared for the coming storm includes solidifying our relationship with Jesus and following the blueprint the Bible gives us to accomplish this relational growth. If I could pick a verse in the Bible that describes the central message to the church in this book, it would be summed up with this admonition.

> Grow in the grace and knowledge of our Lord and
> Savior Jesus Christ. To him be the glory both now
> and forever! Amen. (2 Peter 3:18 NIV)

In this book, we will walk through the steps it takes to recognize and be prepared for the coming storms and to assess and grow into an abiding relationship with Christ. We will also explore the steps to take if you find yourself off course, lost, and tossed on the waves of confusion; deceived and drowning spiritually.

This is not a fair-weather or feel-good book, but I believe it is a message of hope to believers in Christ. I can tell you from personal experience that being unprepared in a storm is dangerous. The storm will take you to places you do not want to go before you even know what has happened. This book comes from that experience. My prayer is that if you, fellow believer, are like me and have lost your way for a moment or are not sure if you may be drifting away to a place in your relationship with Jesus that you did not intend, this might be a beacon to help you to find your way home.

> The LORD makes firm the steps of the one who delights in him; though he may stumble, he will not fall, for the LORD upholds him with his hand. (Psalm 37:23–24 NIV)

THREE

The Forecast

B efore a sailor begins a sailing journey, the sailor checks to confirm that a few very important things have been considered. These include checking the forecast (i.e., the weather in your path, including storms that may be brewing on the horizon); the gear (i.e., equipment to help you navigate your way through the seas, especially the storms); and the anchors (i.e., support to help you stay the course and to maintain your heading). Let's start with a check of the forecast of what's ahead for the church.

The Last Days

The Bible gives us some descriptions of the storm through which we will be required to navigate as we move toward Christ's return and the end of the age. Matthew 24:10–11 (ESV) says, "And then many will fall away and betray one another and hate one another. And many false prophets will arise and lead many astray." He continues in verse 12 of that same chapter to describe a world where the "love of many will grow cold."

Please don't be too quick to say, "This could never happen to me!" I can assure you, our hearts are already colder than you might think. Lest we go too far into the dark, the good news in verse 13 assures us that "the one who endures to the end will be saved."

At the end of each chapter remaining in this section, I have included questions to help you consider whether you can recognize, or perhaps already may have identified, people or situations that may fall into the categories we will discuss. I have also included suggestions for actions that you can take if your answer is yes to these questions.

FOUR

False Prophets

O ne of the great joys my husband and I share is trout fishing on the beautiful river near our home. We have a sturdy fishing boat, but we take seriously the responsibility of keeping a watchful eye on any disruption to the smooth surface of the water. We are watching the waters ahead of us as we navigate the river because lurking underneath what may seem to be a minor disruption of the surface could be a tree or rock. If hit, it could capsize the boat or ruin the motor's propeller. That is a direction disruptor for sure.

As mentioned earlier in Matthew 24, Jesus warned the disciples of false prophets who would come in the name of Jesus Christ, saying "I am the Christ," and they will lead many astray (Matthew 24:4–5).

False prophets and their followers are what we generally know and refer to today as *cults*. *Webster's Dictionary* defines a cult as a religion regarded as unorthodox or spurious.[3] *Spurious* means something that is outwardly similar or corresponding to something

---

[3]   "Spurious." Merriam-Webster.com Dictionary, Merriam-Webster, https://www.merriam-webster.com/dictionary/spurious. Accessed 13 Jan. 2024.

without having its genuine qualities.[4] It is frightening to think of the number of cults that have arisen over the years, all of which promised a better way and a better life for its participants.

In Colossians 2:8 (ESV), Paul urges the church to "see to it that no one takes you captive by philosophy and empty deceit, according to human tradition, according to elemental spirits of the world, and not according to Christ." The phrase "see to it" in the Greek is *blepó*, which means to be on guard, beware, pay attention, or perceive.[5]

In the same way fishers on the river must have watchful eyes on the water's surface to spot any abnormality, believers must also be watchful and aware of the words being spoken in all forms. They must also be aware of practices that are encouraged or required but are contrary to what the Bible teaches. Sometimes it only takes one hit to sink your boat or change your direction.

Similarly, in Mark 13:22–23 (NIV), Jesus says, "False messiahs and false prophets will appear and perform signs and wonders to deceive, if possible, even the elect. So be on your guard; I have told you everything ahead of time." Deceivers are very good at deceiving. If they were easy to identify, I don't think Jesus would have given us this warning. Just as the Bereans examined the scriptures every day to see if what the apostle Paul said was true (Acts 17:11), believers must also not take for granted or assume that every word spoken from the mouth of a preacher, evangelist, or person in ministry is truth. The Bible warns of the things we should watch out for, and it is crucial that we check everything against the Word of God.

---

[4] Merriam-Webster.com, spurious.

[5] *The Complete Word Study Dictionary: New Testament*, ed. Spiros Zodhiates (Chattanooga, TN: AMG Publishers, 1992), page 2062.

I recently watched the documentary *The Way Down: God, Greed, and the Cult of Gwen Shamblin.* It is about a modern-day church that started down the path of mixing faith in God with a weight-loss Bible study program. The documentary reported that, over time, the leader of this church took the position and preached the requirement that its members must be of a certain weight or they would not be considered part of the true church of God. The distortions multiplied from there and arrived at teachings that denounced the role of the Holy Spirit and the Trinity. What fascinated me most about this documentary was that the leader of the church could quote Scripture better than a lot of preachers I have heard. I had to watch it a few times to fully realize the subtle lies that had crept into this church.[6] It was fascinating yet very scary. I wondered if the members of that church were watching for that subtle disturbance on the surface of the water. Did they see the danger that lurked underneath before it was too late?

---

6   *The Way Down: God, Greed, and the Cult of Gwen Shamblin,* prod. and dir. Marina Zenovich, aired September 30, 2021 and April 28, 2022 on HBO.

Questions for Discussion:

1. False prophets can come in sheep's clothing. Have you ever experienced an organization or person that may have preached Christianity but you felt something was off? If so, what was it?

2. The Bible says deceivers can also masquerade as angels of light. Have you ever experienced someone in ministry who seemed too good to be true and made promises that also seemed to be too good to be true? If so, how did you respond?

3. For questions 1 and 2 above, what caused you to feel uncertain about their statements?

4. Can you find anything in the Bible that either confirms or conflicts with those statements?

Suggestions for Action:

1. The role of the Holy Spirit in the life of the believer is to guide and teach. Sometimes, our sense of discomfort with a particular teaching or statement is the Holy Spirit warning us. Do not neglect or devalue the Holy Spirit's warnings. If you have that sense of discomfort in your spirit, pray and ask God to provide you with clear answers.

2. Invest the time to search the scriptures to determine whether the statements or behaviors you have experienced align with the Word of God. The Bible can and should be used to prove itself, so you should not have a situation where the message being preached contradicts scripture in other places.

3. Consult with a trusted pastor, preacher, or other believer to discuss your questions. There is no shame in asking questions and it is important to settle the matter in your own heart and mind about what you have heard.

FIVE

False Teachers

False teachers come in all shapes and sizes with all sorts of teachings that can be contagious. Paul uses yeast to describe false teaching because a little bit of yeast spreads through the whole batch of dough (Galatians 5:9). In other words, a little bit can go a long way to cause people to be knocked off course or to lose their way completely.

What is so dangerous is that false teaching comes from teachers. These people, placed in positions of authority within the church or ministry, have the responsibility to train others to walk a path based on the content of their messages. They have been entrusted with the hearts and minds of others. Woe to teachers who do not take their responsibility seriously (James 3:1).

False teaching is not only about a statement that contains a lie about Christ Himself. It can also include twisting God's Word, or adding to or taking away from the whole truth of the Bible. In 2 Peter 3:15–17 ESV, Peter speaks to the fact that some of the apostle Paul's letters are hard to understand. Peter goes on to say that "ignorant" and "unstable" people "twist" Paul's words to their own destruction. He advises us to be careful not to be carried away and lose our own stability based upon these twisted words. Before we know it, we could have a faith with no clear heading, ever circling and never arriving. Now before you think I am being too harsh, consider that the definition of *ignorant* in the Greek essentially means "unlearned."[7] Further, the word translated for *unstable* does not mean mentally insane; it simply means "unsteadfast."[8] In other words, the false teachers Peter described were essentially making up what they thought Paul's letters meant, and taking their students along with them in that false interpretation as part of their teaching. The students were not secure and steadfast enough in the truths of the Bible to know the difference between what was false and what was truth.

I can tell you from experience that false teachers can be harder to spot than you might think, especially for new believers in Christ who have not received proper training. Many years ago, as a new believer in Christ myself, I decided to attend a Bible study class. It was taught by a person whom I perceived as a pillar of the faith, with years of devoted church attendance and experience teaching classes probably before I was even born. I was sure that I would be enlightened with the deep things of God. I was ready to generally be moved forward from new believer to well-educated scholar on the content of the Bible. What I received were lessons that were not only *not* in keeping with the truths written in the Bible but were so troubling they shook me to the core of my new and fragile belief system. I was shocked that the person I had perceived to be a rock-solid teacher with a deep knowledge of God's Word wasn't.

---

7   *The Complete Word Study Dictionary: New Testament,* page 2015.

8   *The Complete Word Study Dictionary: New Testament,* page 2050.

I was lucky in my situation because my pastor at the time was a wonderful teacher who helped me untangle the knots this person caused. Some are not so lucky. That was an eye-opening experience. It taught me the hard lesson that I needed to be sure I was not simply taking what others were feeding me based on their presumed qualifications. I needed to be reading God's Word for myself and seeking out second opinions on it to straighten out any confusion so as not to alter my course. It is OK to ask questions. Jesus was in the business of answering questions, even those He knew were in the minds of others but weren't spoken. Be careful and be a Berean!

Questions for Discussion:

1. How would you rate your current level of knowledge of the Bible? Are you steadfast in your position on what you have learned?
2. What do you do to check the qualifications of a new teacher or preacher before you sit under their teaching?
3. Do you have a resource or support you can go to with questions?

Suggestions for Action:

1. If you are not confident about your level of knowledge of the Bible, there is no shame in that. It is important to always be aware of this about ourselves, especially if you are planning to attend a new church or listen to a new preacher or evangelist. Everyone must start somewhere, sometime, and today is a good day to commit to growing in your knowledge of God's Word.
2. Small group Bible studies are wonderful avenues for more personal discussion and freedom to be able to discuss those hard questions and to help us grow in our knowledge of the Bible.

SIX

Legalism

The false teachers described in the previous chapter twisted the truth of God's Word. One of the most frequent lies the enemy uses is the false teaching called legalism. In Galatians 1:6–9 (NIV), the apostle Paul was astonished that the believers in the Galatian church were "so quickly deserting" the gospel of salvation through faith in Christ alone for another, distorted gospel that required faith in Christ plus circumcision. In other words, Jesus plus some additional act equaled salvation. Let's put it into a mathematical form to help grasp this concept.

Faith in Jesus + [insert additional action required] = salvation

That is legalism. Legalism is probably the most familiar of any false teaching examples, but it is also the hardest to spot if we are honest. This may step on toes, but when we begin to require that our worship should be limited to certain music, certain hymnals, instruments, or no instruments, we are inviting in a form of legalism. The Lord clearly says He is not interested in our sacrifices and burnt offerings but in the conditions of our hearts (Psalm 51:16–17). In other words, in God's economy, what is happening on the outside doesn't matter so much as what is happening on the inside, in our hearts. What is going on in your heart is what He receives as your worship. Be careful that you are not practicing a distorted faith that includes Jesus + _____ = salvation.

Here is another example. I was raised in a very conservative denomination. As part of my early church training, I received a lot of lessons on the hellfire and brimstone side of God, but not too much of the love of God. I heard the gospel and what Jesus did for me on the cross, but I didn't hear as much about love your neighbor as yourself. In my church, any other denomination was shunned as being completely wrong, regardless of whether it was also a Christ-based church, because those other denominations did not follow the same traditions as my church. Anyone who attended those other denominations was going straight to hell. We were encouraged in a subtle way not to associate with "those people."

Fast forward many years later. I was a divorced, single mom raising a young son. I had the great honor of meeting the man who would later become my husband of now almost thirty years. As we were getting to know each other, I was very impressed that he invited me to his church. We had a long-distance relationship in the beginning, so I traveled to meet him and attend church with him.

As we were driving to the church, I thought to myself that if he attended the denomination of my childhood, I just might marry him on the spot. However, we pulled into the parking lot of the dreaded "other" denomination.

That, my dear reader, was a form of legalism I was taught as a child. To be fair, I am grateful for that dreaded denomination and for my own very conservative childhood church because they both taught the Good News of Jesus Christ. However, we must be careful of teachers, pastors, and congregations bringing other requirements to the table so theirs is considered a right, true, and correctly worshipping church.

Questions for Discussion:

1. God's Word assures us we are saved by grace through our faith in Christ alone. Have you experienced a teaching that expected you to do something else in addition to your faith? Donate money? Abstain from certain foods? Eat certain foods? Perform certain rituals?
2. Do you have established rules in your church or place of worship that must be followed? If so, what are they?
3. Do the requirements or obligations of your church serve to, whether intentionally or not, exclude others from attending?
4. Are those requirements or obligations discussed or described in the Bible?

Suggestions for Action:

1. This chapter may be difficult to resolve in our own minds concerning our church or place of worship and its practices. It is important to not judge too quickly, and it is also important to compare your findings with the requirements of the Bible.
2. Acts 2 provides a wonderful picture of a healthy, thriving church. How does your church compare to the church described in Acts 2? Think about ways that you can help to transform your church into an Acts 2 church.

SEVEN

Gnosticism

Another type of false teaching relates to what is called Gnosticism. Gnosticism is derived from the Greek word *gnosis*, meaning "knowledge." Gnostics believed that all the secrets of God were in the mind, or appeared in an immaterial identity, and that the possession of knowledge was the only requirement for salvation. They also ignored or diminished the significance of the ministry, death, and resurrection of Jesus.[9]

I think we could generally sum up the point of Gnosticism as "bring your brain; no cross required." The Gnostics were trying to convince the Colossian church that their way was better and that intellectualism was all that mattered. The apostle Paul warned the church in Colossians 2:8 (ESV), "See to it that no one takes you captive by philosophy and empty deceit, according to human tradition, according to the elemental spirits of the world, and not according to Christ." He also encouraged Timothy to "guard the deposit entrusted to you. Avoid irreverent babble and contradictions

---

[9]   *The Complete Word Study Dictionary: New Testament,* page 1369.

of what is falsely called 'knowledge,' for by professing it some have swerved from the faith" (1 Timothy 6:20–21 ESV). A little swerve goes a long way toward changing the direction in which we are headed.

I am not condemning the search for more understanding about the things of this world. I am a firm believer in the idea that "knowledge is power." However, this, fellow believers, is the powerful knowledge that God wants us to pursue.

> His divine power has granted to us all things that
> pertain to life and godliness through the *knowledge*
> *of Him* who called us to his own glory and excellence.
> (2 Peter 1:3 ESV; emphasis added)

God is in the details of our beliefs and our understanding of the freedoms, as well as the responsibilities, we have in Christ. He has granted us all we need to live full and abundant lives, and it all begins with our knowledge of Him. He takes seriously what we allow to be accepted into our minds and hearts as truth. He also takes seriously those who are trying to impart false teaching into the minds and hearts of His people. In Galatians 5:10 (NIV), Paul confirmed this point by telling the church at Galatia, "I am confident in the Lord that you will take no other view. The one who is throwing you into confusion, whoever that may be, will have to pay the penalty."

Questions for Discussion:

1. "Spiritual but not religious" is a popular saying these days. How could this be similar in form to Gnosticism?

2. Is there a difference between being "enlightened" versus "Holy Spirit filled"? How could a focus on enlightenment be a false substitute for being filled by the Holy Spirit?

3. During my time in the wilderness, I continued to read my Bible, but I unwittingly allowed myself to gather "head knowledge" instead of using that time for developing and maintaining a Holy Spirit-filled relationship with God. What would be your status today in your Bible reading time?

Suggestions for Action:

1. The Bible is alive and active and judges the thoughts and attitudes of our hearts (Hebrews 4:12). Take time to do an assessment of your devotion time with God. Do you focus on head knowledge only or Holy Spirit-filled communion time?

EIGHT

Deceiving Spirits

In 1 Timothy 4:1, the apostle Paul alerted Timothy to the fact that, in later times, some will replace their faith in Christ with devotion to demons and deceiving spirits. When we first think of "demons and deceiving spirits," we may think of someone dressed up in red with a pitchfork, or perhaps wearing the mask from the *Scream* movies, but this is not the case. Remember that even demons masquerade as angels of light.

It is very important to note that in his letter to Timothy, Paul is referring to the church when he said that "some will replace their faith in Christ." That's right: the bride of Christ will in later times (i.e., a time that is coming) trade her beautiful wedding dress for something counterfeit.

Will these deceiving spirits come claiming they offer a purer religion? It's interesting that in 1 Timothy 4:3 as well as in Colossians 2, Paul describes the message of these deceivers and liars as including twisted forms of godliness such as "don't marry" and "don't eat." Rules and restrictions that equal self-abasement and self-punishment in the name of religion is not from God. Jesus went to the cross to take our punishment, not to make a way for us to punish ourselves.

Paul tells the church in Colossians 2:23 (ESV) that "these [teachings] have indeed an appearance of wisdom in promoting *self-made religion* and asceticism and severity to the body, but they have no value in stopping the indulgence of the flesh" (emphasis mine).

Are we making up our own twisted religion and placing it under the general moniker called Christianity? Perhaps this is the scariest one of all. These deceivers will be coming in the name of religion. There are religious affiliations out there today that operate under the umbrella of Christianity but promote exclusion, deprivation and, as Paul described it, "having the appearance of godliness, but denying its power" (2 Timothy 3:5 ESV).

We must consider how we may be letting our current churches be reshaped into places that require more than simply teaching and sharing of the Good News that is centered in faith, hope, and love.

My oldest grandson, Kael, has a tablet he is allowed to use for a certain amount of time each day. Recently, my husband and I were babysitting our grandsons and Kael was enjoying some time on his tablet. I was busy with our youngest grandson and wasn't paying close attention to what Kael and his papa were doing. They seemed to be searching for an ink pen at Kael's request. Papa found the ink pen and handed it to Kael. Kael immediately started trying to write on the tablet screen with the ink pen. I reminded him that a regular ink pen is not made for use with a tablet. I asked why he needed a pen. He very simply explained to me that the message on his tablet said, "Please enter your pin." He took that to mean he needed to do something with an actual pen. We had a good giggle about that, and I proceeded to explain the difference between a PIN and a pen. I thought of that story in relation to this message about being deceived. He needed a pin, not a pen.

We must be careful to be sure we aren't getting a wolf in sheep's clothing. The Bible says the message of the Good News is simple and we only need the faith of a child to receive it. Faith should not be complicated and neither should be the message of salvation through faith. We only need a simple faith in Jesus and His work on the cross to confirm our destination.

Questions for Discussion:

1. Does your church engage in practices that are disguised punishments for not following certain requirements?
2. Do you feel pressure and stress that if you do not "perform" at a certain level in your congregation that you will be ostracized?
3. Does your church promote love and acceptance of all people, regardless of their background, with no performance evaluation required?

Suggestions for Action:

1. Let's take a minute and let me remind you of just how much Jesus loves you. You are so loved. Jesus has no expectation or desire for your performance. Wherever you are right now in this reading, my prayer is that you feel the love and warmth of Jesus' arms around you. You are not being graded, dear reader-only loved.
2. With a good hug around us, I would gently suggest that you evaluate where your own heart stands if you are in a church that requires some form of performance for acceptance. Are you part of the judge and jury? Or are you standing with the defendant?

NINE

Scoffers

I don't know why the Taylor Swift song "Shake It Off" came into my head as I was about to start this section. The verse I was going to start this chapter is 2 Peter 3:3 (ESV), which says "knowing this first of all, that scoffers will come in the last days with scoffing, following their own sinful desires." The next thing I knew, all I could think about was "scoffers gonna scoff" to the tune of Ms. Swift's catchy melody. Like me, you may now be humming that song as you are reading, but it's OK because I think perhaps in this case, it fits.

Scoffers will come scoffing, but what does that mean exactly? The word *scoffer* in 2 Peter 3:3 is derived from a Greek word *empaiktés* which means a "false teacher or mocker."[10] Jude 19 (ESV) gives us a little more insight into these scoffers by describing them as those "who cause divisions, worldly people, devoid of the Spirit." Their aim is to divide and separate those who are weaker in their faith, who are more easily intimidated by the pressures thrown at them by society and the world.

---

[10] *The Complete Word Study Dictionary: New Testament,* page 2113.

In Romans 16:17–18 (ESV), Paul gives a very clear example of how scoffers may operate.

> I appeal to you, brothers, to watch out for those who cause divisions and create obstacles contrary to the doctrine that you have been taught; avoid them. For such persons do not serve our Lord Christ, but their own appetites, and by smooth talk and flattery they deceive the hearts of the naïve.

As mentioned, the message of the scoffer is one of division and manipulation. However, I think it's also important to focus on the fact that scoffers create obstacles for believers either intentionally or unintentionally. Interestingly, the word translated *obstacle* is the Greek word *skandalon*, from which the word *scandal* is derived. The definition of *obstacle* includes "any impediment placed in the way and causing one to stumble or fall."[11] Imagine that. There are scandals inside and outside the church that cause people to stumble in their faith.

Please listen closely. The enemy, and those he uses, would love nothing more than for believers to hang up their faith and sit the rest of their lives on the sidelines, covered in a blanket of defeat, shame, and confusion.

The enemy uses every trick in the book to try to move us from the truth of who we are in Christ. Our identities in Christ include the rock-solid fact that all our past, present, and future sins are forgiven, and that we are new creations in Christ. He is an anchor for us, securing our position in God's kingdom. We are more than conquerors.

---

[11] *The Complete Word Study Dictionary: New Testament,* page 2274.

I think these tricks are mostly thrown at us as whispers in the dead of the dark night of our souls. There, we are most vulnerable, because, let's face it, just because we are saved through faith, does not mean we automatically have all our stuff together. It's a lifetime of getting our stuff together, and sometimes, we have more bad days than good, so push away those lying whispers.

In today's "one strike and you are out" cancel culture, any misstep or stumble by anyone automatically means he or she must be shunned and never forgiven. Shame on us. Romans 3:23 says that we all fall short of the glory of God. We all are going to need a second chance at least ten times or more before we finish our races. I am thankful that God is a God of second, third, and more chances. I know I have certainly needed more than a few myself and I'm sure that you may have as well.

Here is another case in point. As a divorced, single-mom raising my son on my own, I can tell you that most of the scoffers I encountered were not outside the church, but inside. The condemnation and "down the nose" attitude I received from Christians made me feel like a leper. It also made me believe I would never be truly welcomed in a church because of my past, and that the best I could hope for was to be a second-class church citizen. It took a few years to work through the shame and guilt I felt and learn that God extends forgiveness to everyone who sincerely asks. He wipes those sins away, completely forgotten (Isaiah 43:25). I only wish the church would forgive and forget as easily as God does. When we turn the spotlight on others and focus on the "scandal" of someone's past, we may well be creating an obstacle for someone who is shaky and naïve in his or her own faith. Simply talking about someone's situation in public, whether under the blanket of "prayer requests" or just gossip, has the power to cause division and perpetuate the scandal. We must be careful to understand the power of our words, for good and for bad.

I have heard hundreds of times from people to whom I have tried to share my faith and invite to church that they do not feel worthy to come to church, and that they need to "fix" themselves before they can step foot in the church building. This is the most devastating lie of the enemy so far and fits squarely within the definition of the message of a scoffer that too many people are hearing from those that are in the church. Dear reader, no one has it all together, even those that have their names engraved on the church pew. This lie, this scandal, keeps many desperate souls in need of love and acceptance on the outside looking in. Please join me in spreading the message that Jesus bids us to come, just as we are, and that love awaits those who seek it.

There are two memories that will forever stand out in my mind about the people of my beloved/dreaded denomination. The first was when I started attending that church with my new husband. A dear lady named Linda came up to me with such a welcoming hug and such kind words for both me and for my young son that I was overwhelmed. Just that small word of welcome meant so very much to me, I can't even put it into words. As someone who was on the receiving end of the message of scoffers, this small act of love and kindness from a member of that church was what helped me to keep my foot in the door and to stay.

The second memory was when I was baptized in my new church. I didn't have a Bible of my own, and one day a member of the congregation named Ray came to my house. He said he believed every new member should have a Bible and he gave one to me. I still have that Bible today and it will always be one of the most treasured gifts I have ever received. You see, it wasn't just about the Bible from Ray or the hug of welcome from Linda. The message these two people provided through their words and actions was that I was welcome and accepted, past and all, to be counted as a child of God in the eyes of these dear people.

In Jude 22 and 23 NIV, he appeals to us to be "merciful to those who doubt," to "save others by snatching them from the fire," and "to others, show mercy, mixed with fear." I think he is reminding us that the people on the receiving end of the abuse and division scoffers heap upon them are fragile. I certainly was. They need our help and grace as they are finding their way and strengthening their feet of faith. Maybe this finds you under a mountain of pressure because you are trying to live out your faith with scoffers scoffing their heads off at you. Let me encourage you, in the words of Ms. Swift, to just keep shaking it off. Jude 24 promises us that the Lord is able to keep you from stumbling.

Questions for Discussion:

1. Does your congregation differentiate people based upon their past or present situations?
2. What can you do at your next church meeting to encourage someone who might feel like he or she is on the outside looking in?

Suggestions for Action:

1. At your next church meeting, take a moment to look around the congregation. Do you see anyone sitting alone? Join them. Do you have visitors that haven't been there before? Welcome them.
2. The most powerful way to contradict and defeat the power of the scoffer's scandal is love. Share it.

TEN

Idols, a History Lesson

I thought seriously about titling this chapter "Bright Lights, Big City" because that's what I first think of when I think about idols. Those big flashy things that catch my eye can easily be mistaken for something that might be more important in my life than God. I wish they were that easy to identify.

If you are thinking you have no issue with idols and can skip over this chapter, let me remind you of the words of the apostle Paul in 1 Corinthians 10:13 NIV. He writes, "No temptation has overtaken you except what is common to man. God is faithful; he will not let you be tempted beyond what you can bear. But when you are tempted, he will also provide a way out so that you can endure it."

This verse is quoted in a lot of sermons. I have heard it preached many times. The truth is temptation is common. We are all tempted by one thing or another. No one is above it or immune from it. It's like the common cold. No one is immune, but what may catch my eye and throw me off course may have no effect on you whatsoever and vice versa. Temptation is custom-fit for each person. I think it is critically important we acknowledge, discuss, and teach that, while God provides a way out and a way to endure any temptation, the strength of the temptation of an idol is very great. It's a course disruptor like nothing else. We need help and a solid anchor to hold us secure.

The entire chapter of 1 Corinthians 10 is devoted to the discussion of idolatry. The warnings given to us as believers today are that we are to be very careful in how we conduct our lives and to guard against allowing any form of idolatry in our lives. In fact, the entire New Testament has many warnings for believers to guard against idolatry.

History is always a good teacher. The apostle Paul refers to several historical experiences of the Israelites in 1 Corinthians 10 to teach us valuable lessons about idols. To set the stage, God saw that the Israelites were suffering under the oppression of slavery and terrible treatment in Egypt. God promised to rescue them from the captivity they had been in for 400 years. Fast forward through ten plagues and a mass exodus, we find the Israelites in the desert. Paul teaches us that the experiences of the Israelites took place as examples for us so we will not make the same mistakes they made concerning idols (1 Corinthians 10:6).

One of the first stops on their freedom road was a place called the Wilderness of Sin. While there, the entire congregation of the people grumbled against Moses and Aaron (Exodus 16:1–2). One of the primary causes for grumbling and mistrust of God's provision concerned a basic human need: food. They accused God of bringing them to the wilderness to die of hunger.

God, in His wisdom, gave them manna from heaven to test them to see which way they would walk: in allegiance to Him or not. In other words, He wanted to know if they would trust Him to provide for them and to be satisfied with what He provided. Ultimately, they did not appreciate the manna. They were not satisfied with God and His provision. They wanted something more, and unfortunately, something more is always waiting around the corner to devour us.

What is the history lesson for us, and what are idols anyway? In essence, an idol is anything that becomes more important to us than our relationship with God. It becomes a replacement for God. The Israelites wanted different food. We want things (or people) that bring us joy, happiness, satisfaction, comfort, or maybe escape. Perhaps we want them to fill voids in our lives. First Corinthians 10:23 ESV says that "'all things are lawful,' but not all things are helpful. 'All things are lawful,' but not all things build up." We must be careful what we wish for.

Paul continues in 1 Corinthians 10 to describe the Israelites' experiences. In the next example, we find the Israelites in a literal wilderness in the desert. In Exodus, we learn that Moses left the people at the bottom of Mount Sinai to go up the mountain. While there, the Lord gave Moses the Ten Commandments. The Ten Commandments were to be a set of foundational rules to guide them on how to be in relationship with God and how to stay on the course He laid out for them. Their destination was a physical place called Israel, the Promised Land.

Moses was on the mountain for forty days, and the people grew impatient. Exodus 32:1 tells us they asked Moses's brother, Aaron, for a god that would lead them forward. After a quick golden earring drive, Aaron melted the gold and made a golden calf. What started out as a request for a god to be worshipped in a religious ceremony with burnt offerings and sacrifices turned a corner into something else. With all idols, it never stops at just the original intention or purpose. A worship service for the golden calf then became a party. The people worshipped their new god and then "sat down to eat and drink and got up to indulge in revelry" and one thing led to another, including indulgence in immoral practices (Exodus 32:6 NIV).

The first commandment God gave to Moses was "you shall have no other gods before me" (Exodus 20:3 NIV). Idols are dangerous because, as we saw with the Israelites, one thing always leads to another. Idols plagued the children of God through their entire history. We are wise if we realize that idols are around every corner for us as well.

Questions for Discussion:

1. Can you readily identify anything that assumes a place of greater importance than your relationship with God?
2. Do you rely on other things to comfort, soothe, vindicate, or empower you?
3. How much do you use prayer as a means and resource for what you need or to deal with what you are going through?
4. Would you consider *time* to be a god in your life? How much do you live by the clock, by a schedule, or anything that causes you to mandate your time with God to a place of lesser importance or priority?
5. Is there anything in your life that meets the definition of an idol? If so, what is it?

Suggestions for Action:

1. A self-assessment can be painful, but it is very necessary in this situation. Take time to evaluate what you are prioritizing over your relationship with God.
2. Pray about anything that you have identified that could meet the definition of an idol in your life and re-prioritize your relationship with God as what you seek first and foremost.

My Own Personal Idol

From a navigational perspective, the compass is everything. It is your source of truth when you are trying to determine your direction. According to *Chapman Piloting and Seamanship*, "the marine compass is…the single most important navigational tool on any boat…it guides you on all oceans and waterways in fair weather or foul."[12] Like I said, the compass is everything.

For believers in Christ, our compass is the Bible. The truths contained in God's Word about who we are in Christ and what He has done to make us holy and righteous, forgiven and loved, are the compass that keeps us heading in the right direction.

The marine compass is an amazing tool. It essentially uses the natural force known as magnetism to work. One of the first things any mariner is supposed to do when installing a compass is to zero in the compass. Zeroing in is "nothing more than adjusting the internal compensating magnets [on the boat] so that they will have no effect

---

[12] *Chapman Piloting and Seamanship*, ed. Jonathan Eaton, John Wooldridge, and John Whiting, 69th ed. (New York: Hearst Magazine Media, 2021), page 433.

on the compass when it is installed."[13] In other words, things that may seem harmless enough could impact how well your compass works. They could cause you to deviate from your course if you don't take the necessary precautions to set up your compass so it won't be impacted by any magnetic pull, harmless or not.

Unfortunately, as with a compass, we also have things that can influence our directions. Forces or influences that may seem harmless may be powerful enough to move us off our course. Idols are like that. I think the biggest idols we face are those that seem harmless enough on the outside, but their force and pull can be so strong we can be lost before we know it. For example, my own wilderness experience began with an idol.

I didn't know I was being pulled off course until I found myself being tossed and torn apart. I learned the hard way that my compass (i.e., those truths that would keep my faith in place) was the last thing I thought to take care of.

My story starts at the beginning of what were some of the happiest days of my life. I was a new believer in Christ and so in love with Jesus. I immediately dived into serving in the church. If I'm brutally honest, I was trying to work off the lingering shame and guilt of being a person with a scandalous past. Nevertheless, I had found the love of Jesus, so regardless of all my internal issues, I wanted other people to know about this Jesus too.

I started by teaching Sunday school in the kindergarten class my son was in. I learned the stories of the Bible right along with the children. Over the years, my teaching continued, and I taught every age group up through the sixth grade. Then I moved on to teaching an adult Sunday school class for several years.

---

13   *Chapman Piloting and Seamanship*, 442.

During this time, I developed a friendship with a fellow believer who just loved Jesus. I admired her faith so much. I wanted the kind of vibrant faith she had and to be like her in her walk with Jesus. With her help and mentoring, I came to fully understand and accept God's love for me, past and all. My broken heart for my past sins was healed in part because of this even deeper knowledge and experience of God's love. I know that would not have happened without our friendship. I will always be grateful for that experience.

One of the activities my friend decided to start was a women's Bible study. She and I worked together to facilitate these Bible studies. These were non-denominational classes, and women from all different denominations attended from the surrounding area. It was amazing, and for the little girl that grew up not quite understanding why other people who believed in Jesus had to be shunned because they went to the dreaded denomination(s), this was absolutely the coolest thing I had ever done.

As we have all probably experienced in some way and at some point in our lives, I started to look to my friend as my source of truth, my compass, for all things spiritual. This was a subtle progression over time. It happened in such a noneventful way I did not fully appreciate what I was doing or that I was creating an idol with this relationship, and neither did she. This was not something that she would have ever knowingly advocated. As time went by, the season of our close partnership in ministry came to an end, and I was devastated. My broken heart stemmed from the loss of an idol I did not know I had made.

You see, dear reader, idols are most dangerous and powerful when they come in wrappings of love, with the aim of fulfilling something in you that only God should be allowed to fulfill.

That situation was probably the biggest catalyst for me to venture into my wilderness experience and, to be honest, to stay there. The definition of the wilderness described in the Bible is *eremos,* which means wilderness, desert, desolation, solitude, loneliness, and abandonment.[14] My compass was broken. I picked up the pieces, threw them overboard, and let the current take me and my broken heart wherever it wanted to go. What I didn't know was this current had its own destination in mind. The path to reach the wilderness includes things that are allowed to grow within you but shouldn't.

We will talk more about how I found my way back, but for now, I will leave you with this thought. If you are placing anything or any person above your relationship with God, or if you are placing your hope and trust that this thing or person will do for you what only God can do, consider whether you have created an idol, and flee from it.

---

[14]   *The Complete Word Study Dictionary: New Testament,* page 2133.

Questions for Discussion:

1. How would you describe your "compass"? Does it consist of the Word of God and prayer alone?
2. Have you zeroed in your compass? In other words, have you assessed whether there are any influences or influencers you may have allowed to pull you away from a pure and devoted relationship to Christ alone?
3. Are you taking the word of your influencers over God's Word, our true compass?

Suggestions for Action:

1. If you were like me, this exercise may come as a shock to you that things in your life are not as you thought they were. That's OK. If you feel that this is the situation, it is time to zero in your compass.
2. Make the decision to put away those influences or influencers that are in a position of higher importance that your relationship with God. It will be painful, but worth it.

BOOK II

Assess and Equip

TWELVE

Assessment

The Course

In nautical terms, navigation requirements include both a course and a heading. The course of a watercraft is the "direction in which the craft is to be steered—the desired direction of travel through the water."[15] I tend to think of our courses as being our destinations. They are where we are going. The heading of a watercraft is the "direction in which a vessel's bow points at any given moment."[16] The heading can impact the course at any time. In spiritual terms, our courses or destinations are set when we accept Jesus Christ as our Savior through the grace freely given to all through our faith in Him. No works are required (Ephesians 2:8–9). That destination is an eternity with Him in heaven.

A key differentiator in determining the levels of joy or difficulty we experience on our journey is not with our destination, but with our heading. Having the right heading ensures we arrive at our

---

[15]   *Chapman Piloting and Seamanship*, 50.

[16]   *Chapman Piloting and Seamanship*, 50.

destination using the best and safest route and allows our journey to be fruitful, full, and abundant.

Our destination is set as the body of Christ, but the storms we have discussed previously can impact our individual headings in dangerous ways. Just as sailors prepare for a storm before it reaches them, the storm on our horizon should be taken very seriously and prepared for as well, and the time to prepare is now. We will not have the luxury of fair-weather sailing. For the unprepared sailor, simply believing that plotting a course is the only preparation required, with no regard for the protection or watchful care of their heading, is foolish.

The Assessment

I have lived most of my life with the firm belief that I do not need to read the instructions for anything I need to assemble or use. You can see the results of this throughout my home: desks and cabinets that have been assembled with certain pieces upside down or backward, drawers full of extra parts that have no home because I do not know where they go. In fact, the desk at which I am sitting while writing these very words has a shelf I installed upside down many years ago. It reminds me every day that instructions, guides, and user manuals are beneficial and necessary to fully utilize and enjoy what we have.

We cannot fully appreciate our need for an instruction manual unless and until we conduct a self-assessment to determine how prepared we are for what is ahead. Had I known I would not be able to uninstall and correct my upside-down shelf, I would have taken the time to read the instructions.

In the book of Revelation, the first three chapters describe letters that Christ is writing (through John) to seven different churches. In these letters, He gives an assessment of each church. We can learn a lot from these assessments because each can act as a mirror of sorts to help us to recognize similar characteristics in ourselves. My favorite is the letter written to the church at Ephesus (Revelation 2:1–7). Perhaps it is my favorite because it is the most convicting to me personally.

The church at Ephesus was enduring many hardships while the believers there were working hard. They were toiling hard for Christ's sake and were not growing weary. This sounds like a church that had it all together, right? Sadly, even though this church was standing firm for Christ, being able to identify false apostles and reject them, all while patiently enduring suffering and persecution, their love (i.e., goodwill and benevolence toward others) had been abandoned. In Revelation 2:4, the word for *abandoned* in Greek is *aphiémi*, which means to lay aside, leave, forsake, or disregard.[17] They laid aside their love for Jesus and for others in their striving to do the work of the ministry of Christ.

It is actually not too far of a stretch to realize this same assessment could be given to many congregations all over the world. This assessment could have been applied to me. As a believer, my heart grew cold as I feverishly worked in women's ministry with a broken compass. I was also on the receiving end of scoffers whose behaviors and attitudes revealed hearts that had grown cold as well.

How many believers might be described as Energizer Bunnies for Christianity, but underneath, cold hearts have taken the place of the first love they had for Christ when they were just poor sinners

---

17   *The Complete Word Study Dictionary: New Testament,* page 2053.

in need of salvation? I am confident that most believers would be shocked if they received this assessment about themselves. In the same way that an alcoholic is the last one to admit or realize he or she needs help, the church (both corporately and individually) most likely does not realize it may have a heart problem.

Unfortunately for the world and for the bride of Christ, this heart problem shows itself all too often when we judge others who attend those dreaded denominations, or perhaps those who have not found their faith yet. Perhaps the heart problem becomes evident when we show no mercy for fellow believers who are struggling or who have lost their ways. Just as He did with the church in Ephesus, Jesus asks us to take a step back and remember that place from where we started, where our hearts were warm and we loved much because we knew we had been forgiven much (Luke 7:47). Jesus always has been and always will be more concerned about our hearts and the love within them than the volume of our works.

Where does this find you? For the believer, are you working tirelessly in your church or community for the namesake of Christ, but being rude to your server at the restaurant after church? Are you judging the new believer who comes to your church because he or she started out as drug addict or has a criminal record or is a single mother, or any combination of the above? Alternatively, does this just find you numb, going through the motions of religion and happily sailing along on the sea of oblivion? Before you decide it's time to close this book because toes are being smashed, please know this is not a book on judgment and condemnation. We've all had enough of that from each other and from the world at large.

The point is that to determine where we are as believers and our levels of preparedness for the coming storm, we must honestly assess our hearts. We must be willing to openly evaluate whether we are prepared to survive the storm, or if we might already be lost, tossed, and a little off course already. Let's be real for a minute and be willing to honestly assess where we stand and the conditions of our hearts. Are we hot, warm, or cold?

The following questions are meant to be a tool you can use to assess the condition of your heart toward Jesus Christ today. I ask that before you begin this assessment, please take a moment to pray the following Scripture to the Lord and ask the Holy Spirit to show you the condition of your heart. The Lord already knows and He wants you to see it as well because He loves you. Trust Him with your assessment.

> Search me, O God, and know my heart; test me and know my anxious thoughts. See if there is any offensive way in me, and lead me in the way everlasting. (Psalms 139:23–24 NIV)

Assessment

The following assessment consists of ten questions and one bonus question. The bonus question should not be counted in your assessment tally. It is just something for you to think about. Each question counts ten points for a total of 100 possible points. Determine the number of points you would assign for each question using the scale immediately below. Add the total number of points assessed for all questions and use the grid at the bottom of the page to get an idea of what may be the condition of your heart. Be honest. This assessment is an individual exercise and should not be shared with anyone. This is just between you and the Lord and it is meant to be a safe space.

Rarely	Occasionally	Frequently	Always
0------1------2------3------4------5------6------7------8------9------10			

	Question	Score
1.	How often do you spend time in God's Word?	
2.	How often do you choose prioritizing heavenly things over earthly obligations and desires?	
3.	How often do you go to the Lord in prayer?	
4.	How often do you make a conscious choice not to allow your eyes and ears to take in things you shouldn't?	
5.	How often do you put into practice what you learn from the Bible, sermons, or other Christian content?	

6.	How often do you spend time offering praises and worship to the Lord?	
7.	How often do you look to help the spiritual needs of others?	
8.	How often do you forgive others their wrongs against you?	
9.	How often do you recognize the needle in your own eye before casting judgment on another?	
10.	How often do you have the desire to show the love of Jesus to others?	
	Total	

Cold				Warm					Hot	
0	10	20	30	40	50	60	70	80	90	100

Bonus Questions: Do you feel joy? Are you happy in your relationship with God?

Self-assessments can be tough, can't they? The questions I included are exactly the questions the Lord asked of me, and I can tell you I could not even get to warm. I was shocked, but maybe not really. Do you know one of the key giveaways for my own lack of shock in my self-assessment? The bonus question. I was never so miserable in my life as I was at that point where my heart had grown so cold. That's when I began to realize that my surroundings were in the middle of a wilderness.

I want to remind you this is not a quiz that reflects a pass or fail. It is an assessment to determine readiness. Remember, there is a storm coming. Are we prepared for it? The conditions of our hearts in relationship with Jesus make and keep us prepared. We are saved by faith and not by works.

Finally, I want to share one verse that was a lifeline for me when I fully realized how bad the condition of my heart was.

> A bruised reed he will not break, and a smoldering
> wick he will not snuff out. (Isaiah 42:3 NIV)

Sometimes, whether we stop and take a self-assessment of our own hearts' conditions, or if we fully know we are not where we need to be, I want to promise you the Lord knows where you are and the condition you are in. He is not on a mission to break you. He is on a mission to comfort and restore you, and to remind you of that first, great love: His love. This is the love that sent Him willingly to the cross. Trust Him a little further.

THIRTEEN

The Pattern

"They are like a man building a house, who dug
down deep and laid the foundation on rock. When
a flood came, the torrent struck that house but
could not shake it, because it was well built."
Luke 6:48 (NIV)

My family is skilled in the art of construction. My dad built
the house we grew up in with only the help of one of his
brothers and one of his nephews. My siblings have all worked in
construction at one point or another in their younger years. Two
of my brothers are still in the construction business today. As I
look over at the upside-down shelf in my desk, I realize that I,
unfortunately, am not skilled in construction at all. Thankfully, the
verse above, which mentions building on a rock-solid foundation,
is a comparison statement. It is not a command for all believers to
become actual builders or construction experts. Let's look a little
closer at this verse and the one before it to help us understand what
we want to accomplish with this section.

"As for everyone who comes to me and hears my words and puts them into practice, I will show you what they are like. They are like a man building a house, who dug down deep and laid the foundation on rock. When a flood came, the torrent struck that house but could not shake it, because it was well built." (Luke 6:47–48 NIV)

We dig deep and build on a rock-solid foundation when we receive the words of Jesus, and we put them into practice in our everyday lives. You can't be an expert sailor by only being on the water once a year. You can't be an expert spiritual builder if you are not putting into practice the words of Jesus. There are things we must do as believers every day to be sure we are always prepared.

The sum total of the intended impact of the storm that's coming is to separate believers (i.e., the church), to cause confusion toward each other and within the church, and to cause us to miss the mark on our heading and be thrown off course. The enemy is satisfied if we just build on a sand pile and go about our lives, not realizing the floods from the storm are on the way. It's simple sailing: move the needle just a little bit and we will be shipwrecked or washed away before we know it.

My sister and her husband recently retired to the same area where I live. My brother-in-law spent many years in the construction business, so it was a foregone conclusion they would build their new retirement home themselves. Some of you may be familiar with what is called a barn raising. In our part of the country, it was very common for family and neighbors to volunteer their time and skills to help a farmer build a new barn on his farm. In our case, our family, neighbors, and friends all came together to frame my sister and brother-in-law's new home. We did it in one day. It was the most amazing thing I have ever seen. Everyone worked together, contributing his or her part toward the common goal of building the frame of this house.

You may be surprised that we were able to frame an entire house in one day. What made everything work so smoothly? First, my brother-in-law pre-cut the boards according to their house blueprint. We simply had to fit everything together according to the blueprint.

God has done the same for us. He gave us a pattern, too, and it is in His Word. The Bible is where we find the pattern, the knowledge, and the wisdom to put it all together. In the following chapters, we will discuss a practical guide to being prepared for storms and the right living that goes along with it as prescribed in the Bible. It is sure to be storm proof.

FOURTEEN

Prepare

"**A**n apple a day keeps the doctor away." That popular phrase has been spoken countless times through the generations. The truth that a healthy diet is part of a healthy body applies to all of us.

The implied fact behind this popular phrase is that you must eat the apple every day. Your daily routine must include the consumption of an apple to ensure the doctor does indeed stay away. We are going to use that same analogy as we begin this journey of preparedness.

Window Shopping

One of my favorite movies is the 1970s musical version of *Scrooge* starring Albert Finney. Watching actors with 70s-style long hair playing Victorian era characters is one of the highlights of our Christmas traditions. I first watched this movie in the 1970s when it was released in theaters. My childhood was like the Cratchit family's story because we both lived well below the poverty line. The children standing outside looking in the toy store window was one of my favorite scenes as a child. The images of those beautiful toys were breathtaking to my little eyes because I had never seen so many toys before. Like Tiny Tim, I could not imagine being able to have any of them.

Today, we believers are looking for a consistent, practical way of living out our faith that ensures we are prepared for the storms ahead. However, like Tiny Tim and his sister, we may find ourselves looking through the window at all the things God makes available to equip and prepare us, but we do not go in and take hold of them. The most beautifully wrapped Christmas gift is lovely to look at, but the gift inside does us no good if we never open it. It is the same with that apple. We must eat it to benefit from it.

We will use an acrostic to help us establish a pattern for a daily lifetime routine for preparedness. Can you guess the word we will use? You guessed it: *apple*. Following is a preview for you.

A—Abide
P—Practice
P—Press forward
L—Live
E—Expectantly

FIFTEEN

Abide

The Bible is full of stories about sailors. Did you ever notice that? Starting with Noah in the Old Testament, all the way through the New Testament, we read about men who braved the sea in one way or another. Jesus called fishermen who were also skilled sailors to be his disciples. I think it is appropriate to start this section of our journey with a sailor story.

There once was a fisherman and accomplished sailor named Peter. He had recently changed careers. Peter had traded being a catcher of fish to being a fisher of men at the invitation of Jesus, the actual master of the seas. One evening, Peter and the other disciples were following Jesus's instructions to make a trip across the lake.

As Peter and the disciples were making their voyage, the sea became rough. The waves were high, lightning crashed, the winds were at gale force, and it was night. It is tough to see what's in the storm in the dead of night. They were afraid. All at once, Jesus came, walking on the water. "It's a ghost," they said. "No, wait! Could that be Jesus?"

Brave but a little shaky, Peter said, "Lord, if that's you, call me to come to you on the water."

Jesus said, "Come on!"

Peter stepped over the side of the boat, into the storm. Can you imagine it? Can you see the storm in your mind? Can you see this man stepping out of the comfort and security of a boat and out into the waves? He even made it a few steps before he started to notice the storm around him, the waves, and the wind. He took his eye off Jesus and fixed his gaze on his circumstances, on what was happening to him. He sank.

Jesus was immediately there at his side to pick him up and deliver him safely into the boat. Jesus's only words were, "You of little faith, why did you doubt?" (Matthew 14:31 NIV). I do not get the impression that Jesus was scolding Peter. He was simply saying, "Hey, your faith is weak and it caused you to waver and doubt your security in Me." Peter had not understood what it meant to abide in Christ on that stormy night or he would not have sunk.

John 15:4 (ESV) says, "Abide in me, and I in you. As the branch cannot bear fruit by itself, unless it abides in the vine, neither can you, unless you abide in me." The Greek word for *abide* is *menó* and it means to dwell, remain, to not depart, to continue to be present, or to remain as one.[18] It is a place or state of being that sustains you, provides your every need, and provides a constant path of peace.

When compared to ocean currents, the path of peace from a nautical perspective would be an established path strong enough to keep you going in the same direction, insulated from other events occurring outside of the path of the current. Sometimes the best

---

[18]   *The Complete Word Study Dictionary: New Testament,* page 2199.

sailor is the one who finds that current and lets the water do the work.

Had Peter truly been abiding in Christ that dark and stormy night, he would have realized it wasn't him or his efforts that allowed him to walk on water. It was Jesus. Jesus is our living water (John 4:14), and He is that magnificent current for us to remain in, insulated from events occurring outside of this position of abiding. Our part is to remain in it.

The remainder of this book will be a discussion of some practical tips to help us do that. Let's discuss a little more about the characteristics of abiding. How can we tell if we really are in the current of the Living Water, truly abiding in Christ, and experiencing consistently the abundant life He has made a way for us have? Consider the following as evidence of that abiding. The level to which you are experiencing these characteristics will also help you to determine whether you need to add more APPLEs to your daily life routine.

God-Shine

Abiding is evidenced through spending consistent time in God's Word. I have heard many people ask, "How much time is enough time in God's Word each day?" The answer may sound a bit too simple, but I have found that you have spent enough time in God's Word each day when you feel you have been truly moved by what you read.

When Moses spent time with God, he would return to the people of Israel, his face shining with a glow that came from being in the presence of God. His physical countenance was miraculously changed due to this encounter. The Bible has the same power to impact us for change and for our good. Have you been moved by what you read? Are your attitude, thoughts, words, or actions changed because of the word you read on the page, whether it was one verse, one chapter, or one book of the Bible? Do you have your God-shine on like Moses experienced?

God is ready, willing, and fully capable of speaking words to you that will change your life and your day in seconds. Come to Him without a clock and allow Him to move you through His Word. Be a seeker; revelation comes to those who ask, seek, and knock (Matthew 7:7).

Surrender

I love the old gospel hymn "I Surrender All." Have you heard it before? It was a staple in the church of my childhood, and I still love to sing the words "Humbly at His feet I bow." Part of lasting abiding is to stop resisting the fact that you are a child of God and that your life is not your own. You were bought with a price (1 Corinthians 7:23).

Surrender to the fact that God has a plan for your life. His promises can be trusted as being for you and not against you. Things are only as out of control in our lives as we allow them to be by resisting the sovereignty God has over our lives. That means even in the bad stuff that comes our way when we are doing everything right. Are you surrendering successfully every day to the lordship of Jesus Christ in your life?

Now, don't get me wrong. Surrender doesn't mean slavery. I think the best verse that describes what Jesus had in mind with *surrender* is Matthew 11:28–30 (NIV).

> "Come to me, all you who are weary and burdened, and I will give you rest. Take my yoke upon you and learn from me, for I am gentle and humble in heart, and you will find rest for your souls. For my yoke is easy and my burden is light."

Jesus isn't a slave driver. He offers us a peace that passes all understanding and a freedom to enjoy the blessings of God as His children. There is a difference between surrender and slavery. Which position, either surrender or slavery, does your heart tell you that you are living in?

Obedience

Abiding also comes through obedience to God's Word. It comes through obedience to the next piece of that plan for your life that God reveals to you. It comes through obedience to God's no answers as much as to His yes answers.

Jesus Vision

Abiding happens when we find ourselves looking at others the way Jesus does. Jesus leads with love and sees with love, always. Seeing with Jesus-vision means we are seeing others and loving others in the same way Jesus does. Several of the assessment questions the

Lord put on my heart deal with how we relate to others. I think that is because one of the first things I did on my journey to the wilderness was to completely close my heart to other believers for fear of more hurt and pain.

The Bible says people will know we are the Lord's by how we love. To understand how well you are seeing through Jesus-vision lenses requires a time of reflection. It requires a slowing down of our pace to recognize within ourselves what our outward attitudes and demeanors are toward others. Practicing a self-check of your attitude and actions toward others throughout your day is a very good practice. It can help you stay focused in your everyday abiding. This is critically important when you find yourself in an environment that may include persecution or hostility toward you as a believer.

Praise and Thankfulness

Finally, when you are truly abiding in Christ, praise and thankfulness to God can't help but bubble up to the surface in your attitudes and actions. Jesus said if the people didn't praise Him as He entered Jerusalem that day, the rocks would cry out in praise (Luke 19:40).

Establishing a daily practice of honest praise and thanksgiving makes your day better. Praising and praying to God, worshipping Him, and thanking Him for our blessings and the guidance He gives us is a good practice to help us remember we are never alone in this life, not for one second. The enemy would like nothing more than for us to feel deserted and alone, even in the busiest crowd, because that is where he can do the most damage to our hearts and minds. Feelings of being alone and deserted can allow tiny cracks in our armor. That's all he needs to send those flaming arrows right to those places in us that do the most damage.

Remember the twenty-four-year-old lady who was stranded in the middle of the ocean who I mentioned earlier? One of the key pieces of her plan for survival and rescue was to establish a route that would take her to the major east-west ocean current between North America and Hawaii. She established that plan to go west, farther out into the ocean, because that was the way the strong ocean current was moving. It took her to the islands of Hawaii, where she was rescued. She let the water do the work and so can we. Jesus tells us to abide in Him, the Living Water, because that's where everything is possible.

SIXTEEN

Practice

Philippians 4:9 ESV says, "What you have learned and received and heard and seen in me—practice these things, and the God of peace will be with you." The apostle Paul had it right. Throughout the books he wrote in the New Testament, a common theme is that practice does, in fact, make perfect. We cannot attain perfection, but he urges us to keep working at it.

Such is the life of a Jesus follower. We fall down, are knocked down, or lie down, but we must get up again and keep moving forward and upward. Jesus knew we would have struggles. That's why His inspired Word includes so many verses that encourage us to practice, to take some proactive step or action as a critical part of growing into our faith. Paul tells us to "put off" our old selves and to "put on" our new selves, created in righteousness and holiness (Ephesians 4:22–24 NIV) just like we would put on coats.

The word *practice* in the verse above in Philippians is the Greek word *prassó;* it means to perform repeatedly or habitually.[19] This

---

[19]   *The Complete Word Study Dictionary: New Testament,* page 2254.

means we must make room in our lives for habits that help us maintain our headings. An accomplished sailor checks his or her heading multiple times a day to make sure he or she is maintaining the desired direction. It is the same with us.

In Luke 6:48–49, Jesus teaches about two men, each building a house. The first man dug deep and built his house on a solid foundation of rock. The second man built his house on sand, with no solid foundation. One withstood the storm; the other one didn't. This analogy describes the difference between the person who studies God's Word and puts it into practice in his or her everyday life versus the person who doesn't.

Our blueprint for building our houses on solid rock must include taking in God's Word. It is foundational to our faith and critical to our survival. Reading it, meditating on what we read, and figuring out how to use what we have read to guide our days and lives are critical components of the solid foundation we need as Christians.

Several years ago, I started a practice of writing down verses for some key topics I found helped me in my daily walk with Jesus. I purchased a set of wire-bound index cards, one for each topic, and recorded those verses to use as part of my devotional time. My initial index cards covered the following topics.

- Spiritual disciplines/truth
- Spiritual warfare
- God's promises

The verses I wrote on my index cards for these three topics have sustained me for the last twenty years. I now have verses written on both the front and back of the index cards and I continue to add to them on a regular basis. It is my daily practice to read a verse from each of these topics. God's Word is alive and active. It serves to do many things, including to encourage, guide, provide wisdom, provide correction and conviction, and to remind us of God's love and promises toward His children. It never ceases to amaze me that the verse that pops up for that day is always the verse I needed to hear in relation to what is going on in my life.

I started a set of cards for the topic of spiritual disciplines and spiritual truths because I started to notice just how many verses there are that give us some practical instruction on how to act, how to live, and what to do as part of our training in righteousness. The verses under the topic of spiritual disciplines give me the guardrails in which to move throughout my day. They help to ensure I am walking, talking, and living as Christ would have me live.

If I am being honest, one of the motivations for starting a set of cards for the topic of spiritual warfare was because the enemy was having a field day shooting flaming arrows at me during a particular season of my life. I had the wounds in my heart and mind to prove it. I needed help. The verses on spiritual warfare are my defensive verses. They help me to remember the enemy is already defeated, but still a danger. These verses help me keep my armor on and be prepared for attacks from the enemy. If Jesus used God's Word as His defensive weapon during His temptation in the wilderness, shouldn't we do the same?

The verses I have under God's promise are simply that: promises. The Bible is full of promises God has given us as His children. I think sometimes we forget what an awesome arsenal of strength, hope, wisdom, and love we have in God's Word. It is critical we practice putting God's Word into our minds.

In using God's Word to help in practicing righteousness, I try to make sure I have a verse that will be an anchor for me to stand on for the day. It should be a verse that will hold me secure when difficult things come at me—a reactionary verse. It should be a verse I can use to stand firm, no matter what hits me. I also try to make sure I have a verse that is proactive, meaning a spiritual truth or discipline I can incorporate into my day as a behavior, attitude, or words spoken toward others for that day. Having both a reactive verse that anchors me no matter what comes and a proactive verse I can use that day helps me practice righteousness.

Sometimes, things happen to us or in our lives that completely knock us down. Those rogue waves can hit a ship and sink it or wash people or cargo overboard. This is universal. It happens to everyone. The Bible tells us we will have trouble. It's not a matter of if, but when.

Part of the return journey from my wilderness involved capturing those verses in the Bible that God was giving me to restore me. I have a new set of index cards under the topic heading of Restoration. Hosea 2:14 (ESV) says, "Therefore, behold, I will allure her, and bring her into the wilderness, and speak tenderly to her." God spoke tenderly to me in my wilderness place because, honestly, I don't think I could have handled anything more than that. I was so devastated. He was so tender. These verses are a precious treasure to me because they healed, and continue to heal, my heart.

The journey of writing this book, dear reader, has been the biggest leap of faith I have ever undertaken. Given that I was a tender, broken-hearted wilderness sojourner, I couldn't fathom that this was something the Lord would want me to do. I had to ultimately surrender to His will and His plan for my life. What did

I do? You guessed it. I started a set of index cards under the topic of Surrender. These verses are daily reminders that an attitude and heart of surrender is the only way that truly experiencing the life God has for me will be possible.

I can absolutely promise you that establishing a habit of putting God's Word into your heart and mind every day will change your life, and your day, for the better. Practicing any righteousness apart from what God's Word tells us to do becomes self-righteousness, and there is no set of index cards for that.

SEVENTEEN

Press Forward

In Philippians 3:13–14, the apostle Paul reminds us to forget what is behind us and to press on toward the goal of our relationships with Christ. I love those verses, especially the forgetting part. I love that God gives us permission to leave behind those mistakes, failures, painful situations, and experiences, to simply forget them, as we press forward toward the goal: the prize of our life in Christ.

I think one of the biggest reasons I found my way into my wilderness, and stayed there as long as I did after those painful experiences caused me to throw my compass overboard, was that I forgot to keep pressing forward in my relationship with Jesus. Instead, I drifted, and drifting always seems to go the wrong way.

Adrift

In order to understand the importance of pressing forward in our relationships with Christ regardless of what happens to us, I need to explain the impact that it had on me. The best way to describe how I arrived in my wilderness was the feeling of floating down a lazy river, serene and peaceful. Shocking, isn't it? Now, remember, the catalyst that pushed me toward this wilderness road was a broken heart. I wanted something, some existence, where I would not be hurt or fearful of people, especially people in the church. I wanted somewhere where no one would hurt me and where everything is peaceful and quiet. The lie of the enemy is that this oasis can be found. The truth is that this type of oasis is not the reality of what the Bible teaches. Jesus said in this world, we will have trouble, but take heart, because He has overcome the world (John 16:33).

I allowed myself to drift away from a deepening relationship with Jesus and toward a relationship with the things of the world so eagerly waiting for me. I put my "religion" on autopilot and turned my gaze to other things. I began accumulating material possessions, obsessing about my career and matters relating to the corporate world, blindly staring at a television screen, and scrolling through brain-cell-eating social media. In case you are wondering, the answer is yes, these were all forms of idols to me. I didn't have to run or fight my way to get there. I only had to let go and drift. The undercurrent of this "bright lights, big city" world and my own sin nature took me along on the gentlest ride of my life—in the wrong direction. It wasn't hard; it was easy—too easy. Idols can best be described as warm, soft blankets that slowly smother you.

I was adrift for probably two or three years. A spiritual fog had settled in and around me like that nice warm blanket with chains that continued to tighten around my neck. To be clear, I wasn't in a coma. I was a functioning, church-going, full-time employed person who continued to manage many activities at my local church. From the world's perspective, I was a high achiever. From the church's perspective, I didn't stop loving Jesus, but my heart was closed and cold.

Funny, isn't it? The one thing the world can see as evidence of our love of God and our devotion to Christ is that we love people (John 13:35). That is the one thing I intentionally turned my back on. I wasn't mean or hateful to people, but I definitely was not looking with my Jesus-vision. I continued to have a devotion time each morning, but if I were being honest, I had stopped truly talking to God and actively participating in my relationship with Him. I was going through the motions for that head knowledge but not pressing toward the goal in Christ. I was "phoning it in," as the young people say nowadays.

To my neighbor down the street, or the person sitting next to me in the church pew, I was sure there was no visible change or shift in me on the outside. However, I certainly felt it on the inside, or should I say, I felt nothing on the inside. Something was missing, but I couldn't put my finger on it. I thought what I was doing while going through those motions was enough. I had never been more miserable in my life.

Quicksand

When my misery began to bubble up to my conscious mind, I noticed my situation. The best description I can use to explain how I felt was like slowly sinking in quicksand. I wonder how many of you might say you are in the same place I found myself: playing at some form of religion but not worshiping in spirit and in truth. I was not pressing forward, so I drifted.

I came to the realization I was missing a piece of something I knew would bring all the pieces of my heart, soul, and mind together. Without it, nothing would ever satisfy or bring me true joy and peace—not money, position, family, and certainly not my autopilot religion. I began to frantically search for a rope to pull myself out of the quicksand and above this spiritual fog. I realized then I was not prepared for the storm that had hit me. As I mentioned, my compass was compromised. I also quickly discovered that self-will is not a surrogate for a rope, an anchor, or a compass.

I can tell you honestly I was scared. It shook me to the core of my being to realize I had moved so far away from God without even trying. It was that easy. It also shocked me that all the years of my religious training, and even teaching, had not prepared me to withstand this kind of storm. I was not able to stay on course. I did not recognize this wilderness could result from not being careful with what I allowed my head and heart to believe based upon my circumstances and emotions.

One of the most important and powerful verses we need to take into our hearts and minds is 2 Corinthians 10:5 (NIV). This assures us that we can "demolish arguments and every pretention that sets itself up against the knowledge of God, and we [can and must] take captive every thought to make it obedient to Christ." Had I immediately begun to capture every thought coming into my head after that fateful set of events and stand on the truth and promises of God in His Word, I might not have become lost in the wilderness, or at least not have stayed as long as I did.

You may be wondering what verses in the Bible would have helped me in this situation. I can tell you already what they are because I have read them a million times over the years.

> Dear friends, do not be surprised at the fiery ordeal
> that has come to test you, as though something
> strange were happening to you. (1 Peter 4:12 NIV)

So then, those who suffer according to God's will should commit themselves to their faithful Creator and continue to do good. (1 Peter 4:19 NIV)

Great verses, aren't they? The problem is I had read them many times, but in my time of greatest heartbreak, I failed to internalize and practice them as I should have. The Greek word for *commit* in verse 19 above is *paratithémi;* it means to deposit or entrust (as a trust or for protection).[20] Instead of putting my heart in a lockbox to ensure I was protected from any further hurt or pain, I should have entrusted my heart, my mind, and my feelings to Jesus and let Him help me work my way through the situation. Pressing into Jesus is the only way to maintain your heading.

The definition of "press on" in Philippians 3:14 is the Greek word *diókó,* which means to run after, to run swiftly in order to catch a person or thing, or to press on.[21] The hard lesson I learned is that if we are not pressing forward consistently every day, especially when we face fiery trials, we drift and find ourselves lost and tossed about with no anchor to hold us secure. I also learned that part of what helps us remain focused on pressing forward is to let go of the past, forget what lies behind, and commit our hearts, even when they are broken, to the One who loves us most.

Course Corrections

Remember the book I mentioned in previous chapters about the young lady who successfully navigated the open sea after a hurricane

---

20   *The Complete Word Study Dictionary: New Testament,* page 2233.
21   *The Complete Word Study Dictionary: New Testament,* page 2089.

almost destroyed her boat and high-tech equipment? She performed one practice on a daily basis, and sometimes multiple times per day. What was it? She checked her navigational heading. She used the position of the sun, the speed of the currents, and a handy piece of navigational equipment that didn't require electricity, to determine where she was and how fast she was going.

I have realized through my experiences in coming out of the wilderness that we also need to check our headings every day. We must recenter ourselves using the equipment God has given us: the Bible and prayer. Psalm 32:8 assures us God will instruct us in the way we should go, and He will counsel us with His eye upon us.

The Bible is alive and active, according to Hebrews 4:12. It cuts through our human logic, fear, and frustrations to speak to us about the heart of issues that may be course disruptors. God is in the details of our lives, both personally and professionally. Whether you are in the work force, serve the church in some capacity, or are a stay-at-home parent or spouse, God is there with you. He is intimately aware of everything that comes your way, both good and bad, both happy and frustrating.

One thing I have learned is that stress and worry are absolute course disruptors if there ever were any. Why? Stress and worry are primary triggers that can cause us to let go of our anchors. People frustrate us with their attitudes and actions that are not Christ-like. People hurt us in the name of righteousness.

Course corrections must be part of our daily routines. We must build in moments to check where we are, to recenter ourselves, and to make sure we refocus our eyes and hearts on God and on His Word.

In the first three chapters of 1 Peter, we receive a lot of guidance and encouragement in the face of hard times. Persecution of the early church was rampant, and believers were discouraged and even fearful. Peter encouraged believers not to be surprised at what was happening. We should not be surprised either. This is a tough world. It's even tougher to maintain our sense of peace and stability in such unstable times.

That is why looking for those anchors in God's Word is so critical to our survival. God gave us a map in His Word to help us navigate this life. Take up the Word daily and recenter yourself.

EIGHTEEN

Live Expectantly

H ere we are with the last two letters of our APPLE acrostic:
Live Expectantly. There are really two parts to this chapter.
The first part is probably what you think it will be: we should live
in expectation of the Lord's imminent return. We don't know when.
However, if we are living out our faith on a daily basis, abiding
in Christ, practicing His righteousness in our lives, and pressing
forward, it doesn't matter whether Jesus comes tomorrow or in one
hundred years. We will have done our parts.

In Matthew 25, Jesus tells the parable of the ten virgins who
were waiting for the bridegroom. As they waited, five wise maidens
prepared their lamps with extra oil and five foolish maidens did
not. When the bridegroom came, the five who were not prepared
were left scrambling to buy extra oil and did not accompany the
bridegroom into the wedding feast. You see, dear reader, we must
prepare and remain prepared every day, living expectantly that the
Lord Jesus will return. Are you ready?

This brings us to the second part of this last chapter. In Jeremiah
1, God commissions Jeremiah to go where the Lord would send him

and to speak the word God gave him to speak. God gave Jeremiah a mission to, in some cases, uproot and tear down, to destroy and overthrow, and in other cases to build and to plant.

You and I have decisions to make. To ensure we are prepared when the Lord comes, and to ensure we do not lose our way and find ourselves in the wilderness, we must tear down the idols we have allowed into our lives. We must uproot every argument from false teachers, false prophets, and scoffers who have exchanged the truth for lies. All these arguments are against the knowledge of our God. Do you see why in so many different places in the Bible we are told to grow in our faith, increase our knowledge of God, and practice righteous behaviors and attitudes? These practices are our anchors, dear reader.

We absolutely must build on a solid foundation, which is the Good News of Christ Jesus and the salvation He offers us. We must plant God's word in our hearts every day. We must continue to uproot, tear down, demolish, and overthrow every lie of the enemy and even every lie our own broken hearts may ask us to believe.

NINETEEN

Conclusion

My wilderness experience brought me to my knees. Thankfully, I stayed there. In desperation, I finally, thankfully, sincerely called out to Jesus for help. I confessed my sin, and I asked for forgiveness. I kept asking for help until I felt the Holy Spirit say, "I am here."

The next step I took was to dive deep into God's Word to remind myself of the promises of God and that they are truly for me, just as they are for you. God's Word does not change. It is an anchor. Promises such as "I will never leave you nor forsake you" (Joshua 1:5) and "nothing can separate us from the love of God" (Romans 8:34–39) were Scriptures I had known for years. I needed to remember them afresh and apply them as I would apply a healing salve to a wound.

I needed to know God still loved me and was not condemning me for what I had allowed to happen to our relationship. The enemy certainly worked very hard to convince me my standing as a Christian was ruined and I would never be the same. In one sense, he was right. I won't ever be the same, but I also believe God doesn't want me to be the same either. Our heavenly Father wants you and me to be prepared, to equip ourselves with the knowledge of Him, to understand what this life is, and to do what the Bible tells us to do to be prepared for those storms.

My heavenly Father tenderly reached down and pulled me up out of the quicksand I was slowly drowning in. He promised me He would not bruise or break me further. He reminded me of that wonderful, life-giving love He gave His life to secure for me.

My heavenly Father also tenderly reminded me that fear and unforgiveness were chains that would keep me in my wilderness. Matthew 6:15 (NIV) says, "But if you do not forgive others their sins, your Father will not forgive your sins." What I learned was that my healing could not be complete until I forgave as the Lord had first forgiven me.

Am I over it? No. Am I back to normal? No. I am a recovering wilderness survivor and a practicing forgiveness giver. I still have a lot to learn about building on that firm foundation so this never happens again.

Where do you and I go from here? Let's recap what we've learned. First, we must acknowledge, recognize, and accept the forecast of the storms the Bible makes clear are in our future as children of God. Second, we must assess the states of our hearts and our relationships with God. Where does this find you? Has your love for God grown cold?

Third, we must look around and pay attention to what we are allowing to influence and shape us. Do you see scoffers, deceivers, false teachers, or prophets? Be a Berean and beware. Where do you stand with idols? Is there anything in your life you have placed in a position of higher importance than a relationship with God?

Finally, we've learned it is a lifelong endeavor to develop and grow our relationship with Christ. It takes daily attention and prioritization, practice, and a secure attachment to the anchors God in His wisdom has given us. With these things in mind, we endure, continuing to look to our faithful Creator and to do good. We continue growing in the knowledge of Jesus Christ, loving others as Christ loved us, and forgiving others as Christ forgave us.

With great love and much compassion, our Father in heaven looks down on His children who are in wildernesses, whether by drifting slowly or marching into them intentionally, or by being shoved into them through circumstances that were a bit too overwhelming. He knows the wilderness is not where we belong. He has made a way for us through the wilderness to return, be healed, be brought to safety, and be strengthened along the way.

For all who have found themselves on the wilderness road, and to all who may not realize they are in the wilderness, I pray this book accomplishes what the Lord intends for it in your life. Wherever this may find you, He knows where you are and He will show you the way to come home.

> We must pay the most careful attention, therefore,
> to what we have heard, so that we do not drift away.
> Hebrews 2:1 (NIV)

ACKNOWLEDGMENTS

To Alice Aldridge: you prayed me all the way through and all the way home. My debt of gratitude for your commitment to prayer can never be repaid.

To my Jesus, for Your glory and for Your church.

BIBLIOGRAPHY

Chapman Piloting and Seamanship. Edited by Jonathan Eaton, John Wooldridge, and John Whiting. 69th ed. New York: Hearst Magazine Media, 2021.

The Complete Word Study Dictionary: New Testament. Edited by Spiros Zodhiates. Chattanooga, TN: AMG Publishers, 1992.

Merriam-Webster.com Dictionary, Merriam-Webster, https://www.merriam-webster.com/dictionary.

Oldham Ashcraft, Tami, *Adrift.* HarperCollins Publishers Inc., Digital Edition May 2018. Kindle.

The Way Down: God, Greed, and the Cult of Gwen Shamblin. Produced and directed by Marina Zenovich. Aired September 30, 2021 and April 28, 2022 on HBO.